QR CODES
IN EDUCATION

Copyright 2013 David Hopkins

Discover more from David Hopkins on subjects from eLearning, Blackboard, Digital Literacy, QR Codes, Social Media, MOOCs, Technology Enhanced Learning, eBooks, etc. on his Technology Enhanced Learning Blog – www.dontwasteyourtime.co.uk - or connect with David through LinkedIn.

What is being said about 'QR Codes in Education:

All you ever wanted to know about using QR codes in Education is in this book. It takes you from the very basics of what these delightful square barcodes are, how to view the information they link to, how to easily create your own and, most importantly, a vast array of ideas on why you would want to use them! Whilst not a newcomer to QR codes, I came away from reading inspired and with new ideas of how QR codes could be used to enhance learning and teaching."
Sue Beckingham (@suebecks), Educational Developer, Sheffield Hallam University

"The information is concise and user-friendly. The 'Planning, Creating, and Monitoring your QR Codes' chapter offers everything you need to get going with QR codes. Because of David's extensive experience, you won't have to learn the hard way. He's made it easy. The book is well-balanced - but keep this in mind, David's examples and suggestions for using QR Codes in Education are very persuasive."
Brian Bishop (@bbishop262), CEO, Efficacy Experts

"David's book is a great place to begin for those educators who wish to start using QR codes in their classroom. The book begins by explaining what QR codes are and then delves into examples of use in education and Libraries. A veritable treasure trove of inspiration, the book should be read for this [last] chapter alone and I will be definitely trying some out."
Julian Wood (@ideas_factory), Sheffield Primary School Future Learning Technologist

Technical Reviewers

Many thanks to the following for their review and comments during the various stages of writing this book:

Sue Beckingham, Educational Developer, Sheffield Hallam University (@suebecks)
An Educational Developer and Associate Lecturer at Sheffield Hallam University with a research interest in the use of social media in higher education. Sue is also a Fellow of the Higher Education Academy and the Staff and Educational Development Association.

Zak Mensah, Digital Manager, Bristol Museums, Galleries & archives (@zakmensah)
Zak currently works as a Digital Manager For Bristol Museums, Galleries & Archives where he is responsible for everything digital. He has previously worked for the University of Bristol (JISC), the University of Leicester, and also runs his own digital studio, www.tribehut.com.

Paul Simbeck-Hampson, Social Business Catalyst (@simbeckhampson)
Paul is a Social Business Catalyst based in Bavaria. His work with QR codes is an extension of a bigger interest in the 'Internet-of-things', especially with how technology can support connectivity and access to knowledge.

Craig Taylor, eLearning Specialist (@CraigTaylor74)
Craig has honed his facilitation skills delivering face to face learning events across a range of sectors including the British Army, Rail and Nuclear industries and Financial Services. He now concentrates in raising the profile of how current and emerging technologies can be used to enhance and enrich the learners experience whilst adding demonstrable benefit to the business.

CONTENTS

INTRODUCTION

If you didn't already know, this is a QR Code:

Scan it and something wonderful happens – you're transported from the page, an offline 'analogue' resource to an online digital world. Often you won't know what you'll get until you scan the code but, if the person who developed the QR Code has done their job properly, you should have a good idea as they have given you a reason to scan it: a video, a download, a voucher or discount code, etc.

This book is about using QR Codes to bring the online digital world and the offline paper-based world together in an educational setting: classroom, library, school, university, field trip, book club, etc.

I have written this book for anyone who is involved or interested in making learning more fun, more interactive, more dynamic. Through this book you can gain an understanding of what QR Codes are and how they can be implemented and used in an appropriate manner in your learning environment:

These little black and white squares have appeared everywhere from billboards at the side of the road, roof tops, cola cans, buses, magazines, etc. So why not in your library, textbook, assignment, project, or classroom display? The ability to use them to direct students or colleagues to online resources (presentation slides, websites, video, book review, etc.) is powerful and engaging and, when well implemented, can offer a level of interaction and engagement. It's not about what they are but about how we use them and what they can offer in an educational setting.

Using computers and technology in educational environments can be exciting and challenging. Implementing QR Codes within your student's learning is just that: exciting to see how students of all ages use and interact with them, and a challenge to make them usable, informative, applicable, and appropriate.

This book draws on established examples from the commercial and corporate world as well as from established users of QR Codes, from all levels of education; from primary schools up to Universities. Not only will you find examples of how QR Codes have been used but you will find out how you can design, create, and implement your own QR Code treasure hunt, library resource, student group work, orientation activity, conference or event feedback, etc.

Background

I first came across a QR Code in 2008 on the side of a Pepsi Cola bottle. I didn't have a clue as to what it was or what I was supposed to do with it, but it said that by scanning it I could access individual content, prizes, and games.. So I started searching. At this time there was little information available other than basic examples of QR Codes used in marketing. A few leading educators I follow on Twitter had starting writing about them and their impact on classrooms or educational uses. It all sounded promising but, as I didn't have a smartphone, I ignored it and did something else, probably what I was planning to do in the first place before becoming distracted.

About a year later I got my first smartphone, an iPhone 3GS. Shortly afterward this, when trying to find things to do with it, I remembered the QR Code. I downloaded a scanning App and started to see what all the fuss was about. Admittedly the first attempt didn't go too well but, as I was about to learn, it was less about my mistakes and more about the mistakes made in the implementation of QR Codes.

From the first scan I wanted to learn more. More importantly I didn't want to commit the same mistakes I observed when I first scanned one. I searched and clicked my way around many early websites and blog posts supporting QR Codes (some positive about the possibilities of QR Codes, while others bemoaned their gaining popularity). I learned that the best looking QR Code was made from the shortest amount of information / characters as possible (shortened URL), to leave a large amount of white space around it to help with scanning, to position the QR Code in a prominent position on the page and to not hide them in a corner, to explain what you user should do with it, and why they should scan it (discount, information, game, etc.).

I also learned that they were not, at that time, widely known or understood and that I'd have to repeat the same conversation many times:

> *You: What's that?*
>
> *Me: That's a QR Code.*
>
> *You: A what?*
>
> *Me: A QR Code. It's like a barcode (you know, like on the side of your cornflakes packet) but it can contain more data than just a number string.*
>
> *You: Data? Like what kind of data?*

Me: Like phone numbers, web address, email addresses, simple text.

You: Why would you want one of them?

Me: It's a quick and simple way to link the printed world with the online electronic one. Use your phone to scan the QR Code and be directed to a website or a contact number from a business card. Like that.

You: Why would I want one of those?

Me: How many students do you get asking for you to email them the links or resources from your lecture? How many complain you didn't give them enough time to copy the web address? Why not let them scan the QR Code at the end of the lecture and they'll get the resource or download right there, right then?

You: Really, as simple as that?

There were often more elaborate versions of that conversation, some went on for months (off and on)! After a while this got really tiring.

So it was time to do something about it. I blogged and tweeted about QR Codes and made a right nuisance of myself. But I also had a lot of different and more supportive discussions around their use. This led me to develop blog posts and ideas around using QR Codes in and out of the classroom, which I shared online through my Technology Enhanced Learning blog and through Twitter (@hopkinsdavid). By 2010 I was known for my work with QR Codes and was invited on many occasions to explain and demonstrate their power and abilities. My blog posts are regularly re-tweeted and mentioned or copied and have had over 50,000 hits to date (May 2013 - thank you Google Analytics for helping me find that).

In collaboration with Dr Milena Bobeva at Bournemouth University I submitted and published posters for the 2011 Bournemouth University Enhancing Education Conference and the 2012 the Association of Business Schools Learning & Teaching Conference. In January 2012 I devised and delivered, with Dr Bobeva and Andy Ramsden from University Campus Suffolk, a workshop funded by the Higher Education Academy that would "offer the opportunity for knowledge transfer and development of new skills and ideas through networking with people interested in QR Codes as a new form of communication channel."

http://goo.gl/nuSwg
2011 Bournemouth University
Enhancing Education Conference

http://goo.gl/iosdi
2012 The Association of Business Schools
Learning & Teaching Conference

http://goo.gl/9o0GM
2012 QR Codes in Higher Education
Higher Education Academy Workshop

QR Codes and Web Links

The point of this book is to show how scanning a QR Code can bring the digital world to the printed paper one ... so this book is full of QR Codes for you to scan.

 I do not expect you to scan them all but you can use the QR Code in the manner in which they are produced ... to link the paper offline world to the online digital one, where resources are colourful, moving, etc.

As I will explain in the chapter on **"Planning and creating your QR Codes"** all my QR Codes have a URL underneath them – I consider this good practice and enables those without a scanning device to still use the resource by typing this link into a browser and access the resource (device and platform independent).

Where I link to online resources I use a *shortened URL*, created with the Google shortening service – Goo.gl http://goo.gl. There are many benefits to this tool, the most pronounced is the aesthetic nature of how the links look and 'flow' on the paper and in relation to the text it supports: short, neat, tidy, and in a uniform way across the whole book. If I were to use the full URL for each link then some would be long, some short, (some very long indeed) and therefore make the layout of the text and paragraphs messy and broken. It's all about the aesthetics – all Goo.gl shortened URLs are the same uniform length, 19 characters.

Image source: Ali Galehban http://goo.gl/fdEUW

Book QR Codes

In this book I will always put the QR Code after the explanation or description. Sometimes I reference a resource or article in a section where it is not always appropriate to split the content with the QR Code – in these instances the QR Code will be as close as possible to the relevant content as I can get it, without disrupting the reading experience.

I mentioned earlier that I'll be using the Goo.gl URL shortening system. Apart from the aesthetics and statistics it affords me, the greatest advantage for me here, in this book of QR Codes, is that when you add ".qr" to the end of the URL and Google will create a QR Code for the shortened link. Nice! So, using the shortened URL - http://goo.gl/P93fv - and adding the ".qr" to the end to make http://goo.gl/P93fv.qr will create the following QR Code:

http://goo.gl/P93fv
David Hopkins' books

If you want to take the QR Codes further with Goo.gl, as I have been doing with all the QR Codes in this book, on posters or promotional prints, then you'll need a larger QR Codes than Goo.gl initially provides you with. This is how:

When you view your QR Code, as created by Goo.gl, the full URL in your browser address bar will have a whole lot of code in it, like this:

Change the section that reads 150x150 (the pixel size of the QR Code) to something larger – up to a maximum of 540x540. You then get a larger QR Code that will give your scanning audience a larger QR Code (and therefore a clearer and 'cleaner' scan) which will work from further away:

Book Videos

There are some great resources available on YouTube that are good (and bad) examples of QR Codes that have been produced and distributed. These videos are not only from official channels but from the wealth of really good 'amateurs' (I say amateur with tongue-in-cheek as these can sometimes be more accurate, interesting, and informative than professionally generated ones). I have again used shortened URLs and QR Codes for you to scan or type into your browser and watch online.

WHAT IS A QR CODE?

I am not going to go into great technical detail about what a QR Code is, how it is constructed, or where they came from, as it is assumed that because you are reading this book you already have a basic understanding of what one is, or don't care and just want to get on and use them.

I will indulge myself, however, and give you a *brief* re-introduction. What you see next is a 2-dimensional (2D) Code, a "Quick Response" Code, a **QR Code**.

With an appropriate application on your mobile device you can scan it and be directed to a digital resource. What this digital target will be is determined by the person who created the QR Code and what they chose to direct you to once you've scanned it.

It could be:

- A website or web page,
- A YouTube video,
- Contact details,
- Phone number,

- A pre-formatted text / SMS message.

If you scanned the previous image you would be directed to a page dedicated to resources on QR Codes on my Technology Enhanced Learning (TEL) blog www.dontwasteyourtime.co.uk. However, it is not a QR Code that is made of the link above, it is a QR Code made from the shortened URL http://goo.gl/M9MTf - something I'll explain more about this in the **"Planning and creating your QR Codes"** chapter.

So ... what is a QR Code? According to the Wikipedia entry a QR Code is

> *"... a type of matrix barcode (or two-dimensional code) first designed for the automotive industry. More recently, the system has become popular outside of the industry due to its fast readability and large storage. The code consists of black modules arranged in a square pattern on a white background."*

http://goo.gl/f2i9h
Wikipedia: QR Code

Again, you ask, what is a QR Code (in plain English this time please)? It is simply a matrix of black and white squares that, when scanned, decode the information into a series of alpha-numeric characters. Most scanning applications ('Apps') will then interpret this series into an Internet address (and display it), or a message, or SMS / text message (number and / or text content), or the contents of a VCard.

The following two videos are a good introduction to QR Codes, what they are, and how you can use them. Whilst they are not set in or around education environments you will gain a valuable base-level introduction from which you can develop your own ideas for their use:

http://goo.gl/RG5xz
YouTube: QR Codes in Plain English

http://goo.gl/UOQFF
YouTube: What is a QR Code?

EXAMPLES OF QR CODES

QR Codes as a technology was quick to be adopted for marketing and commercial purposes, and it is some of these I want to share with you now as examples of how QR Codes can successfully be used to link the printed media to online, digital world.

All of the below examples have a marketing orientation to their use and purpose, but development in this field has helped the rest of us to learn from their successes (and failures) and develop & direct our own experiences on how QR Codes can be used in an educational environment.

Example 1: For the DVD release of the film '28 Weeks Later' a billboard was put up in London showing a QR Code and web address, and nothing else. Those who scanned the QR Code or visited the website had information on the film, could watch the trailer for the film, and get more details on the DVD release.

http://goo.gl/ygQc4
1. 2007: 28 Weeks Later DVD

Example 2: The Pet Shop Boys (UK) released a single called 'Integral' criticising the British National Identity Card. The single was accompanied by a video complete with a QR Code linking to the critique and "content about issues of civil liberties". In some respects this is a really poor use of QR Codes as it requires the scanner to have two devices available: one to play the video, and the other to scan the QR Code.

http://goo.gl/kCwE4
2. 2007: Pet Shop Boys music video

Example 3: This was the first instance of a QR Code that I encountered was on the side of a Pepsi Cola bottle. Scanning the code would launch you into a mobile website for mobile games, prizes, information, etc. This was possibly the first main stream use of QR Codes, with a reported 400 million cans and bottles tagged with QR Codes and competition details. We must also remember that this soon after the iPhone was released and before the smartphone market really took off, so it was a bold move for a top-level confectionary company like Pepsi.

http://goo.gl/Ko8pD
3. 2008: Pepsi Cola mobile phone code campaign

Example 4: Static billboard displays are all well and good, but when you want to do something different, there is little room for innovation. In 2010 Calvin Klein used a billboard in downtown New York City and enticed passers-by to scan the QR Code to "get it uncensored". Get what uncensored? That was the incentive for this advertising success: what better way to encourage scanning other than the person thinking they're getting something 'naughty' ... which is what they got.

http://goo.gl/4q4V6
4. 2010: Calvin Klein Jeans

Example 5: Promotional posters are placed everywhere in the run up to a film's release, and making yours stand out from the crowd is not always easy, but the posters for the 2010 release of 'Iron Man 2' used a QR Code to link the poster to interactive content, film stills, and watch the film trailer online while still out and about.

http://goo.gl/I60xx
5. 2010: Iron Man 2 poster

Example 6: To try and engage shoppers on their daily commute, in a city (Seoul) where commuters didn't have time to visit a shop to buy their groceries, Tesco devised the 'virtual' store by placing real-size billboards on the subway walls commuters could scan a QR Code for a product, add it to their online shopping basket and complete the transaction, all underground. The basket contents would then be delivered within the day. This example (use the link provided) has a good video attached to it showing the project and results, well worth a couple of minutes to watch.

http://goo.gl/U60by
6. 2011: Tesco virtual store

Example 7: Bus timetables on bus stops and lamp posts had scannable QR Code for live bus information, on what bus on what route is expected for the bus stop where the QR Code is scanned. This service has now been replaced with a mobile app and mobile-friendly website for live bus information and location-finding software, but the exercise was considered a success at the time with over 5,000 scans per month.

http://goo.gl/vbx1K
7. 2011: Bus Timetables

Example 8: When Betfair sponsored the UK Volleyball team of Zara Dampney and Shauna Mullin they placed a QR Code quite literally on their bottoms! When scanned (if anyone got close enough) the individual would have access to the Betfair website for free registration and a free bet.

http://goo.gl/0btaZ
8. 2011: Volleyball sponsorship

Example 9: As someone who has bought and sold property recently the most difficult thing to do, when driving through the area you like, is to find out the details of the house you like. By including a QR Code on the property board you could quite easily scan and view the property details, and, if you like it, contacts the vendors agents to arrange a viewing. If the QR Codes are not placed on a property board then a carefully placed QR Code on the property particulars that are mailed out could link to the property online or, even more useful, to Google Maps so the scanner can get easy directions to find the property to view it.

http://goo.gl/zcqoA
9. 2011: Real Estate Particulars

Example 10: 'Simon on the Streets' put the QR Codes to clever use during their winter 2011 campaign. By putting a QR Code on a piece of cardboard, the charity placed the board, along with bedding and empty bottles, around cities in places where homeless were known to sleep rough. Passers-by, who wanted to donate or give money to the charity supporting those who sleep rough, could donate to the 'Just Giving' page by scanning the QR Code and making an online donation, quick and easy.

http://goo.gl/uy2Sz
10. 2011: Simon on the Streets Charity

Example 11: To promote the EURO2012 tournament Coca Cola placed QR Codes on their cans and bottles to link to exclusive videos of the event, both in the event run-up and during its progress. By modifying the QR Codes location, without the need to change the QR Code (which you can't once it's been printed) the campaign can be changed and updated as the tournament progressed.

http://goo.gl/H49Ji
11. 2012: Euro2012 Cola Cola campaign

Example 12: San Francisco gourmet sandwich shop use QR Codes on table tops for patrons to scan and order their sandwich online through the digital menu and, when it's ready, the patron goes up to the counter to pay and collect. The next generation of this process would be to enable online payment too, so the patrons order and pay online.

http://goo.gl/EFqKc
12. 2012: Mobile Payment

Example 13: Mixing both humour and important health information together is a unique and comical method, and very cleverly done. The QR Code in the full size image is scannable, and well worth scanning.

The cartoon says "The flu vaccine has come a long way. Time was, we gave you a needle. Then there was a nose spray. Now I just show you this for a few seconds.

http://goo.gl/ONvRp
13. 2013: Health notice

Example 14: In the event of the emergency services needing to get a trapped individual out of a vehicle Mercedes-Benz are making this process safer and easier with the inclusion of QR Codes. Emergency services can scan the code at the scene of the incident and get an instant schematic of the vehicle and where important cutting point, fuel lines, electrical wiring, etc. are so they can avoid any further delay or injuries.

http://goo.gl/dNgQ3
14. 2013: Mercedes-Benz QR Codes

EXAMPLES OF QR CODES IN EDUCATION

QR Codes offer you the ability to save time, save paper, and encourage students to think beyond the traditional 'paper' vs. 'digital' media. QR Codes, as I've already mentioned, can help facilitate the link between paper and online worlds.

Image Source: David Hopkins http://goo.gl/SLlhA

Question:

"Why not just give people a URL to type / save?"

This is a question I've heard people say. Well, even when using shortened URLs it can go wrong if it is written down or typed incorrectly or too quickly – if the URL has an upper-case 'O' it could be seen as a '0' (zero) and therefore the link is broken. The same is for '1' (one) and a lower-case 'L' in some fonts.

Why make it more difficult for someone to find you online or to view or interact with your hard work – use a QR Code and, so long as you've tested it properly and it works, make the link YOU want them to use? Admittedly, by using a QR Code on its own you are also preventing non-smartphone users from viewing the work or resource but, if you see the chapter on "**Creating and Monitoring your QR Code 'Campaign**", this does not have to be the case.

Below are some examples of the different uses and different contexts QR Codes can be used in.

In the Classroom

QR Codes in the classroom could be a great way to pass information from one source to another: from teacher to student, from student to student, and even from student to teacher. I have also heard of QR Codes being used by students to showcase their work to parents, School Governors, and passers-by who walk passed the School windows! What an excellent way to include the wider community in the students' work, brilliant!

Posters / Wall-art (tutor)

Do you want to produce resources that are engaging and serve to entice your students into finding out more? QR Codes can offer this functionality. As students are often involved in topic or project specific work you can help them find information using your own posters (examples below) whilst also acting as a demonstration to the students on how they can use a QR Code in their own work.

Example 1: A single poster with pictures of important world leaders, pre-and during World War II, and a QR Code associated with each linking to a YouTube video synonymous with the individual and their leadership or presentation style.

http://goo.gl/FXvSp
1. History / World War II – Famous speeches

Example 2: A single poster, again, for a classic novel (Jane Eyre) with QR Codes linking different resources school children need access and exposure to, like details of movies made on or about the novel, links to online resources putting the work and author into historical context, author biography, downloadable eBook, etc.

http://goo.gl/KnSCn
2. English / Literature – Book resources

Example 3: What an excellent use of QR Codes! A (large) poster that shows the periodic table with a QR Code for each element that links to a YouTube video showing the characteristic properties of the element.

http://goo.gl/5F5Xi
3. The Periodic Table (video)

Example 4: Designed to help students understand and master a variety of sport skills, these QR Code-enabled posters add extra educational value to the printed resource

http://goo.gl/3KKOF
4. 'Skill' Posters

Posters / Wall-art (student)

Where your students produce work that is to be put on the wall or displayed somewhere why not get them to create a short video of them introducing it, what they did and how they did it, and any other little bit of information that they want associated to the work. Upload the video to YouTube or Vimeo (or other online video hosting service) and display a QR Code on or near the work – this way the student is always on hand to explain their work, project, etc. to whoever wants to hear more about it.

This can work in the classroom, for the other students to explain to each other and the teacher about their work, or can be used (when the work is displayed facing out of the class) by students passing it in the School corridor. This is also a really good idea if the work is displayed in windows or display areas in the School for parents or prospective parents to view.

Example 5: Use QR Codes on a poster in the classroom to highlight states and places of interest, either current or historical, or (in this case) official state websites. Students can then use this as a base for their studies and return to it for more information and to add their own research.

http://goo.gl/KXnVW
5. Geography map

Student Portfolio

Students will create a lot of resources, they will be engaged in numerous projects, and they will produce a wealth of information and knowledge that ought to be shared – not only with their peers but also the rest of the School.

Example 6: "So often, children create digital texts and produce work using technology that is 'forgotten' or 'left behind' after it is created. QR codes help document these activities and keep a record of the rich learning opportunities that children experience, including providing evidence of the skills they apply in the process."

http://goo.gl/29YcV
6. Student Portfolio

"Word Wall"

Expand the vocabulary of your students by creating a 'word wall' – each poster covers a different element of a project (e.g. science terminology) and the students can scan the QR Code on the project to visit a dedicated page for that poster / word and therefore expand their knowledge of that scientific term (including video and / or animations that demonstrate the real-world context of the term).

Example 7: QR Codes, pasted to a wall or poster enables students to expand their knowledge of scientific vocabulary, terminology, experiments, or processes through the scanning and resources they can find.

http://goo.gl/uclUx
7. Lakeview Students – 'Word Wall'

Science Fairs

Often work or projects displayed at Science Fairs are complicated and in of explanation, and the student(s) involved in the project are not always present to explain about their work. By creating a short video and having this available on a scannable QR Code this is not a problem.

If the project is a difficult one, and a demonstration is prone to problems working (we've all been there) then a QR Code linking to a video of the project working could be a great way to showcase the project, working, and in the best possible way.

Presentation Slides

Example 8: If you want your students to access your slides or an alternative resource think about how a QR Code could facilitate this. Place a QR Code on the final slide in your presentation and leave this on the projector screen as the students leave the room – they can scan it as they pass and have the slides (SlideShare – www.slideshare.com - is a good online store for PowerPoint and PDF presentation files) downloaded by the time they get home or to the next class.

http://goo.gl/kK9mV
8. QR Codes in the Classroom

Equipment

If you use specific or complicated equipment then a carefully placed QR Code near it can link the user to an online tutorial to help them be safe and operate the equipment in the appropriate manner.

http://goo.gl/YDQZH
9. Creating and using an 'Art-cube'

Example 9: An 'art-cube' is just a cube / dice with images on each side instead of numbers, and in this instance QR Codes are used to enhance the images or the theme of the cube. You can put a QR Code on the cube as part of the work or use a QR Code to link to the online art-cube generator and the individual cube as part of the student's portfolio of work.

Museum & Art Exhibition

Make a mock art exhibition for your students – display noted, famous, or obscure paintings around the classroom with a QR Code located next to each one. Students, once they have scanned the QR Code, get an introduction to the painting and artist and then given a task to complete before coming back to present their findings to the class.

Example 10: Homework is assigned prior to a school visit – each student group is assigned one artist and asked to produce a short piece of work detailing a little about the piece of work, using a QR Code so others can read their work. After the gallery visit the groups have to scan each other's QR Code and try to decipher the writing and figure out which painting or sculpture it refers to.

http://goo.gl/zah7U
10. Lesson Plan – art exhibition

Example 11: QR Codes at the 'Tales of Things' exhibition at the Petrie Museum enable visitors to read further information about the artefacts and, more interestingly, leave their own comments and thoughts. Add to this the ability to share their thoughts through social media and you suddenly enable a much wider appreciation of the art and enhance the experience for the visitors.

http://goo.gl/pHX1L
11. Interact with the exhibits

Audio & Podcasts

QR Codes can direct the scanner at any online content, so why not create an audio recording or podcast and use the QR Code to send the scanner to your audio homework?

Example 12: If you are involved in any form of language tuition then getting your students actively engaged in the subject is key, whether it is learning a new language or improving their first language. With recordmp3.org students can record and save their work and publish it with a QR Code. Great for students to add to posters or homework where they describe their work.

http://goo.gl/xj7Od
12. Audio-based homework

In the Library

Libraries are, or have been, all about paper-based resources. This is no longer the case.

Image Source: James Clay http://goo.gl/VaWal (CC BY-NC 2.0)

Book Review

By including a book-specific QR Code on the cover or inside the main cover the reader is able to access further resources appropriate to that particular book. The QR Code directs the reader to online content (study guide, student blog, student review, teacher introduction, etc.) before needing to make a decision about loaning the book.

Example 13: This great video from Jarrod Robinson highlights the varied used of QR Codes in libraries, especially placing QR

Codes on book covers and directing the scanner to a review or alternative resources they ought to consider.

http://goo.gl/tGbvk
13. QR Codes on Library Books?

QR Code Reader / Station

Example 14: Not all School libraries allow a mobile phone inside, which will cause problems if you want to use advances in technology like QR Codes. One way round this is to provide a dedicated work station that is equipped with a small webcam, a set of headphones, is connected to the Internet, and some basic instructions. This will still enable students to scan and view the digital resources associated with a text, but it will not be a truly 'mobile' solution.

http://goo.gl/L6zak
14. What's B&W and scanned all over?

Student Blogs

If you're lucky enough to have students interested in writing their own blog, or participating in a class blogging project, then each post is a valuable 'document' of them and their learning and writing journey. With a QR Code for each post added to the text, poem, or book it is about placed in the book the next person to read it has the opportunity to read a critical review or blog post about the book / poem and have another view from which to work with.

In the Field

If you know that your students will have access to the Internet whilst outside the classroom, either on your School's property or on field trips, and then why not see about using QR Codes whilst you (and them) are out and about?

Use QR Codes to create and run a fun way to get children outside and active. If they have mobile devices, or access to one temporarily, then they can take part in a treasure hunt in or out of class time.

Example 14: This community project aimed to deliver audio content through the use of location-specific and accessible QR Codes on the Cotswold Canal. The podcast material contained interviews with locals who described their experiences and history of the location, and these interviews were made available through the scanned QR Codes or, in some cases, re-enacted by performers in a narrative story.

http://goo.gl/MNzPXQ
14. Audio trail

Example 15: Hide the QR Codes around the designated location (school, building, village, etc.) each QR Code contains a question relating to the study topic. Some questions test existing knowledge while some need a little thought or further investigation. Answers to the questions, once all QR Codes have been found and scanned, are written down and handed in by the student group for checking and awards.

http://goo.gl/4ayHK
15. How to set up a treasure Hunt

Examples 16 & 17: Using QR Codes around a geographical location, in this instance a small village, to help primary school-aged children (5-7 years old) to find out what it was like to live and work in the village 100 years ago. From this the children were then also able to see how the village was shaped and how it grew in time, with the people in it. Using stories from the community on how it was and what it is like now, a great many photographs and biographies were found and created for the safari. With the QR Codes placed strategically around the village visitors, friends, and locals are all able to find out about its history, traditions, culture, working- and family-lives.

http://goo.gl/bsqYR
16. QR Code Treasure Hunt
(without Internet access)

http://goo.gl/tIswX
17. Scavenger Hunt

Example 18: This project from JISC was involved in "linking learning to location" through the use of QR Codes, but was fundamentally grounded in the pedagogic use of the technology and the student engagement with it. The project had three elements; extended exhibition space, interactive historical tour of Ipswich, and an orientation treasure hunt for new students.

http://goo.gl/Okynn

18. Extended exhibition space, interactive historical tour, and treasure hunt

QR CODE READERS / SCANNERS / APPS

The world of Apps is forever changing, and the list below is just a snap-shot of what is available at the time of writing (2013).

Note: This list is not exclusive is an updated list from my post from May 2012 and the list generated for the January 2012 Higher Education Academy workshop 'QR Codes in Higher Education'.

http://goo.gl/lsO33
QR Code reader Apps

Smartphone readers / Apps

Scan (iOS – Free) - Billed as the "the fastest, simplest and most user-friendly QR Code and barcode scanner available" it's certainly the quickest to be ready to scan a QR Code from launch, but is not always able to scan the QR Code if you don't hold the camera square on to the QR Code, and in good light. I use this one frequently and the 'history' feature is a good way to revisit websites you were directed to if you haven't got access to the QR Code anymore.

QR Code Reader from Kaywa (iOS – Free) – The Kaywa website was the first I found and used to create QR Codes, and this App is still a firm favourite of mine to scan them as well. While some more complicated or 'altered' QR Code designs don't work on other Apps, they nearly always work with this one. A very valuable App to have on your iOS-enabled device.

QR Code Reader and Scanner (iOS – Free, Android - Free) - Scan QR Codes you find on your travels, in magazines, on posters, etc. with this useful and free app. Use the history feature to view / review your past scans but make sure the QR Code is on a flat surface and in a well-lit area (and not on a glossy finished page, it'll prove difficult to scan otherwise).

QuickMark (iOS - £0.69, Android - Free) – The only QR Code App I've paid for but it is by far the most powerful of all the scanning Apps I use, enabling you to scan and create QR Codes on your device (based on URLs, contact details, plain text, etc.) or you can use a photo you've saved in your camera roll to scan after the event, if you're in a hurry. It is also worth checking out the QuickMark website if you use other types of mobiles as they have developed the app to work on other OS too, as well as a QR Code reader desktop solution! For the price it is well worth it, in fact if it could only recognise the QR Code quicker and start quicker than this would be the best app I've downloaded.

Bee Tag (iOS – Free) - BeeTag will scan a QR Code as well as a normal code (as do the others above) but this app also acts as a price checker on normal barcodes. There is no history feature with this app but the list of available options when you scan a QR Code is impressive, giving you the option to view the code, view / show the URL, save or send the URL to an email or SMS recipient, or save it to a favourite list.

Unfurl (iOS– Free) - This is a new one to me and I'm still trying it out but so far it's quite good. It's quick to launch and only has one function: to scan the QR Code. The advantage of this app though is that it traces the codes path "so you know whether or not it's safe before visiting the underlying web site." I'm not sure how it does this, or based on what it makes the %'age analysis for its trustworthiness, reliability, privacy, and child safety, but it is a good reaction to some comments about QR Code 'honesty' that are doing the rounds at the moment – source: Mashable QR Code Security.

http://goo.gl/S8QKN
Mashable QR Code Security

QR Droid (Android – Free) – "Change your smartphone into a powerful QR Code, Barcode, and Data Matrix scanning utility. Import, create, use, and share data in a matter of taps. This intuitive, full-featured and multi-language QR utility will change the way you interact with QR Codes and their smart actions and activities."

Google Goggles (Android – Free) – "Search by taking a picture: point your mobile phone camera at a painting, a famous landmark, a barcode or QR code, a product, or a popular image. If Goggles finds it in its database, it will provide you with useful information. Goggles can read text in English, French, Italian, German, Spanish, Portuguese, Russian, and Turkish, and translate it into other languages."

QR Code Scanner (Blackberry - Free) – "Now scan the QR codes accurately and fast with your phone any time using this application. Scan accurately and fast with QR Code scanner.

Simply point it at the QR Code you wish to scan, hold still and in a few seconds the code's contents will be displayed on your BlackBerry®"

QR Code Scanner (Blackberry – Free) – "Turn your phone into a QR Code scanner and start connecting the physical world to your mobile device. Want to scan QR Codes with your phone? Tired of using other scanner apps that fail to scan a QR code with your phone's camera? Problem solved with this QR Code Scanner."

QR Code Reader (Windows – Free) – "QR Code Reader quickly scans QR codes and saves the coded information on your Windows Phone, to be viewed at your leisure."

Scan (Windows Phone – Free) – "Scan is the fastest & most user-friendly QR Code and barcode scanner available. It's just simple QR Code and barcode scanning the way it should be. Open the app, point the camera at the code and you're done! No need to take a photo or press a 'scan' button like other apps."

Desktop readers

QR Codes are not just for those with smartphones and mobile devices. As we've seen in the examples of QR Codes in libraries there can be plenty of use on desktop (or rather non-mobile computing devices).

Note: You will, obviously, need a webcam installed to your computer in order to view and scan a QR Code. It is also a requirement that, in order to install these programmes to your computer you will have or need administrator access. You may need to check with your IT Services for this access.

I would also recommend a certain amount of caution when thinking about using these systems, and certainly you should test thoroughly before putting them somewhere public for use. I had to move the webcam and adjust the lighting considerably to get a simple and clearly printed QR Code to scan. Environmental considerations need to be made as well as the instructions you'll need to give the your students need to be very clear in how to get them to work, and how to position the QR Codes in order for them to be successfully scanned.

QReader: http://dansl.net/qrreader/
Not an easy programme to install and get working quickly but, once working, is very useful and fairly stable. You will need to experiment with QR Codes to get the lighting and position of the QR Code central to the viewing area. The settings will need changing so that a successful scan will automatically open the resource: if you don't do this you may not know if the scan has been successful.

QuickMark: http://www.quickmark.com.tw
From the same people as the smartphone App, QuickMark offers a desktop scan and QR Code creation tool too. Very easy to install and get working, this is not as sensitive as QReader or bcWebCam.

Screen shots of QuickMark QR Code desktop scanner
Image source: David Hopkins http://goo.gl/FmQGR

This is the only programme that can read a QR Code from your screen, not only through the viewfinder on your webcam – so any electronic document, web page, etc. that you find it can scan.

QuickMark is by far my preferred desktop scanner, purely because of the ease of use and the ability to create QR Codes as well.

bcWebCam: http://www.bcwebcam.de
The simplest and smallest of the programmes this one is very good. Be aware that on occasion it started giving all instructions and help in German instead of English, but a restart soon sorted that out.

Screen shots of bcWebCam QR Code desktop scanner
Image source: David Hopkins http://goo.gl/FmQGR

QR CODES – SUCCESS OR FAILURE?

No technology is without its problems or its detractors, and if there weren't a few from each for QR Codes then I'd be worried. QR Codes have come under fire from all directions for all sorts of reasons: some valid and well-presented and others more of a rant and less well structured.

Probably the biggest problem with QR Codes is not actually with the code or technology itself, or how we use them. It's got more to do with the march of progress, that QR Codes have been overtaken by developments in mobile computing and the ingress of technology into our everyday lives.

QR Codes started to gain traction in the marketing world with the gaining popularity of smartphones and tablet computing devices with both adults and children. With more devices available and getting cheaper, either owned individually or provided by the school / university, the greater the availability of the technology needed to scan and interact with these funny black & white squares. What has, for some, signed the death warrant for QR Codes is the development of Augmented Reality technology and improved features and specifications of the latest smartphones and tablet devices?

B.L. Ochman writes that QR Codes had fundamental problems that were more related to their implementation rather than the technology itself. More often than not "the codes were deployed poorly in spots where they couldn't be scanned, like billboards, or -- perhaps lamest ever -- on license plates. Some QR Codes require a proprietary scanner good only for that code, which few people are likely to want to download."

http://goo.gl/iB0aB
B.L. Ochman: "QR Codes Are Dead,
Trampled by Easier-to-Use Apps"

Ochman does go as far as to indicate what brands *should* be doing if they want to maximise QR Codes, and her suggestions include the kinds of things we've covered in some form or another in this book already. There are:

- Make it easy for consumers to use.

- Explain how it works, in clear, concise language.

- Employ it only when it can add something unique to the user experience.

- Make sure content or ads that contain it won't be put in places where cellphone service is unavailable.

- Make the apps available only for situations when using them makes sense.

Alex Kutsishin is less than generous with praise for QR Codes, saying that "if there ever was a technology that was frustratingly unpopular despite its true potential to improve the way consumers and businesses interact, it would be the QR Code." Alex does at least give the QR Code some respite by saying it "may have been ahead of its time" but has an eloquent argument that the lack of industry standard for the code itself and lack of standard scanning application on the multitude of devices available meant that it would never be scanned on a whim. The user would have to have made, at some point, a very definite decision to find out about the code, download a scanning app, and try it out.

http://goo.gl/b5qmI
A. Kutsishin: "Why QR Codes don't work"

The problem with QR Codes (YouTube):
Scott Stratten makes a funny and informative plea in this video about using QR Codes and 'unmarketing'. Take heed, as Scott's viewpoint is mirrored by quite a large proportion of people who come across QR Codes.

http://goo.gl/0xXe7
S. Stratten: "The problem with QR Codes"

Our purpose, and that of this book, is to make sure we use QR Codes appropriately, that we implement them when we need them, that they work (on all devices and in all physical locations), and that they add value to the individual who needs to scan it!

Why QR Code Campaigns Fail?

Despite the above 'reservations' of QR Codes the main point for their failure I see all too frequently is not the code or the technology itself, it's how it has been implemented. A poorly designed or implemented campaign will not work, no matter how good it looks. This is the same for your own QR Code as it is for a large commercial operation.

Why put a QR Code on a poster or billboard you intend to put underground ... where there's no mobile signal? But what about the QR Code itself? Even if it is underground you could still scan it and access the link / resource later when you have a connection. But only if you can see it to scan it, yes? In the same vain why would you put a QR Code on your School or University's football teams' shirts when (you hope) they'll never be standing still long enough for anyone to scan them?

Have you seen a QR Code on a poster by the side of the road, by the side of a train track, even on the Tube (underground)? It's not only silly to put them on a poster destined to be underground (does anyone get a phone signal down there?) but it's even more insulting when they're barely visible. Yes, it has happened, and the Paper.Blog website has a good selection of them for you.

http://goo.gl/DHtyf
Paper.Blog: "QR Codes Explained:
the good, the bad, and the ugly"

What about the idea to trail a QR Code banner behind an aeroplane and fly above a town, or a QR Code advertising a cure for nasty bed bugs (not itself bad, but on a train where everyone will see you scanning it … ?), or on your headstone / tombstone? Check out the following two websites for more examples of QR Codes failing … or rather the implementation of the QR Codes failing:

http://goo.gl/5XzA7
10 Funniest QR Code fails

http://goo.gl/tSMw7
Three brands that failed with QR Codes

Dan Wilkerson has written about his list of "5 Reasons QR Code Marketing Is Broken (and How to Fix It)", about the failure of QR Code-enabled marketing campaigns, and why they failed. These points are just as valid when looking at the implementation of QR Codes in and around your classroom. These are:

http://goo.gl/9dSGL
D. Wilkerson: "5 Reasons QR Code Marketing
Is Broken (and How to Fix It)"

Worthless Content: If there is nothing to explain to the consumer what they will gain from scanning the code, why should they? Provide a contextual reference on what the QR Code is for, what the user can expect to get when they scan it, etc. Make sure the target for the QR Code is mobile ready / enabled and will work on the devices your audience is likely to use, be it smartphone, tablet, etc. (and don't forget to try it with different scanning apps on different platforms, they don't all work all the time).

Awareness: Few people understand or know about QR Codes; therefore you are already limiting your market and target audience. Hell, just give them some simple instructions on what to do with the QR Code: "Scan this code with your smartphone QR Code scanner to get ... ".

Value: Unless your QR Code is going to somehow enhance someone's life or give them something they wouldn't otherwise get (or want). If you're planning a marketing campaign then the QR Code needs to offer something new and unique: exclusive discount or content not available anywhere else. You need to make the process of 'finding your phone, unlocking it, finding the QR Code scanning-App and activating it, waiting for the camera to initialise and focus, scanning the QR Code, decoding it, and then waiting (again) for the website or resource to load' worth it. Very little is worth all that hassle unless it's really important to the audience. That's where unique content will play a large part.

Location: Yes, you can put your QR Code on everything and have it everywhere, but as we've seen above there are some places it's just not worth putting them. Like on billboards / advertising boards at the side of a motorway, on posters underground, a building's roof, a dog's jumper, etc.

Design: Many consider the black and white squares ugly (I quite like them). While the majority of QR Codes are just standard black and white, some people have been creative and used Photoshop and other tools to make them look pretty and inviting too!

Check out some of the tools I list in the Planning, Creating, and Monitoring, your QR Codes section on quick and easy online tools that will help you with a few 'different' takes on the basic QR Code design.

If you want to see more examples of QR Codes being used badly then the WTFQRCodes website is worth a look. There are plenty of examples of QR Codes failing, and the list (and pictures) is still growing.

http://goo.gl/GIwYh
WTF QR Codes website

Why QR Code Campaigns Worked?

Let's not be too hasty and consign QR Codes to the technological rubbish heap. As a technology it is not flawed, but it may have missed its opportunity for mass-market coverage. QR Codes that did well or were deemed a success were ones that were able to capture the eye or imagination of the intended audience, whether it was sports fans, brand aficionados, loyal music lovers, etc.

I don't want you to think badly on QR Codes, so here a few success stories not mentioned in the initial list of QR Code examples:

By frosting a QR Code onto the side of pint glass Guinness made a bold statement – the QR Code was only scannable when the glass was filled with a dark, creamy liquid, like Guinness. It wouldn't work with larger or light ales, only the dark stout. The QR Code pointed to a social media campaign enabling you to share your pint on Twitter, FourSquare, Facebook, etc. as well as unique coupons and vouchers.

http://goo.gl/Q0RBz
Guinness Pint Glass

Japan is one market where QR Codes was a success, the public lapped up everything that had a QR Code plastered on it, and Audi were keen to take advantage of this when they produced this 'world's largest QR Code' (video) to commemorate 100 years of Audi.

http://goo.gl/BYspC
Audi (Japan) QR Code

QR Codes were placed on different cheese products that, when scanned, displayed a mobile-friendly website and a recipe for using that particular product.

http://goo.gl/DwBtA
Kraft Foods

As we have seen in the chapter on websites to help you create your QR Code you don't have to stick with the mundane black and white versions. Have a look at some of the following valid and scannable QR Codes, it is possible to make them really rather colourful and wonderful:

Home Box Office (HBO)

HBO (US cable TV provider) used the above QR Code as an enticing, and fairly grim, introduction to their new vampire-and-gore TV series 'True Blood'. It is still one of the most repeated and blogged about 'pretty' QR Code.

Corkbin (US wine merchant) used this QR Code to direct buyers the mobile website for information and ordering details for their inventory.

Corkbin (US Wine Merchant)

By rounding the edges and adding graded colour you can make the QR Code a thing of beauty. The above example is for the Los Angeles Convention and Visitors Centre (mobile-ready) website. No idea what they are ... scan the code and find out!

Los Angeles Convention and
Visitors Centre

Monica Burns has written a great article outlining the five reasons she loves working with QR Codes, and these echo my own thoughts and feelings about the technology, and how we use it (note the key here is always *how* we use the technology, not the technology itself).

Long web addresses: As I mentioned in the introduction to this book, long web addresses (URL) are messy and obtrusive in the flow of work or text. Mistakes can be made when taking down long URL, which are made even worse if the text on the screen or journal / paper is small and not easy to read. If you use presentations and project it to a screen then your audience will not always know how long they have to make a note of the URL and make silly mistakes.

http://short.url

Image source: Ali Galehban http://goo.gl/fdEUW

Tell your audience at the beginning of the presentation you'll be showing them a QR Code (or two, with accompanying shortened URL for those who don't want to, or can't scan it) and make sure you leave it on the screen long enough for them to scan or write it down. You won't have to pause as long as for a lengthy URL.

Direct access: If you leave your class to find the resource you've just shown them, and they use a search engine, how certain are you they'll find the one you wanted them to find, and that they'll not find some uncomfortable or adult content instead? Encourage the use of shortened URLs and QR Codes in your practice to direct students to the right resource. They can always go off and search for other related resources on their own, and should be encouraged to do this too, but at least in this respect you are being responsible and taking care of their online experience.

Go one step further than this and ask students to go and find their own related or similar resource and present it back to the class through their own self-created QR Code?

Time: As with the shortened URL you are saving time by offering the QR Code to be scanned. You could argue that the process and time it takes to 'find your phone, unlock it, find the QR Code scanning-App and activate it, wait for the camera to initialise and focus, scan the QR Code, decode it, and then wait for the website or resource to load' is equal to the time taken to write down a long URL. But the scanning activity eliminates problems with errors in typing.

Ease: Creating a QR Code is easy, and quick. Planning the QR Code and what it will do, and how it will be used, takes longer, but the steps to create the code are quick and easy.

Routine: If you've never used QR Codes before you do have a steep learning curve, as will your students when they use it for the first time. But if you work at it and get the use of the QR Code right you will all enjoy the benefits and it'll be easier and quicker next time. As always, if you get the students involved they'll be the ones who will take the initiative and have the imagination to try new things with it. Try it and see.

http://goo.gl/IUYQg
M. Burns: "5 Reasons I Love Using
QR Codes in My Classroom"

PLANNING, CREATING, AND MONITORING YOUR QR CODES

There are a number of websites that will create your QR Code for you, most of them for free. Some will just give you the QR Code and that's it. Some can give you options for enhancing colours, or adding a logo, or full statistical analysis of where and when it was scanned.

Outlined below are some of the better websites I have used. You can also use some of the mobile 'Apps' (see the previous chapter) to create codes on the fly – I have highlighted this feature in the 'App' list, if it is available.

Before you start

Before creating your QR Code (or codes) you need to consider where you will put / display them as well as the resource you will link the QR Code to:

- Is the resource behind a security login? If so how will the person scanning know this and pass through the security?

- Is the resources mobile ready / friendly?

- Do you have the space to print and place an adequately sized QR Code so your audience can scan it?

- Do you need to instruct your audience on what a QR Code is and how they can use it? If so, do you have the resources in place to help them with this, or do you need to develop these too?

- If you are linking to an online resource make sure you have a shortened URL for it. Test it, and then test it again with another scanner or device to make sure it works!

- Define your 'purpose'. "The more your QR code enhances or streamlines the lives of customers, the more engagement you can expect. As such, the most important step in making your QR campaign a success is to think clearly about the purpose of your code." Chan continues by saying "The clearer you are about the purpose of your campaign, the easier it will be to discern whether your goals have been achieved."

http://goo.gl/eySGt
H. Chan, 2011: "5 Steps for a Successful
QR Code Marketing Campaign"

- Deliver value and a favourable user experience – Jeff Korhan writes that "what is most relevant is that you as the [owner] are the one who gives your codes value. They are just tools, and how you use the tool determines the value derived from it." He continues by saying that "QR codes can serve a specific use for you, mostly as a lead generation tool. How are you doing your lead generation now? If you can use what is working for you now and make it better, more attractive or easier with QR codes, you are probably on the right track."

http://goo.gl/rGOfS
J. Korham: "5 Steps to a Successful QR Code Marketing Campaign"

In a very un-scientific experiment I printed the two QR Codes you see below side by side and clipped the paper to a board and scanned them (the content of the QR Code is beneath). Each was printed the same size, 3 inches wide:

http://www.dontwasteyourtime.co.uk/conferences/bu-enhancing-education-2011/
BU Enhancing Education Conference, 2011

http://goo.gl/nuSwg
BU Enhancing Education Conference, 2011

The content of the QR Codes above are very different: the first is made up of the full web address, whilst the second is the shortened URL of the same address. They may look quite similar to you or I but to a scanner the resolution (size) of the QR Code means it can be easier (or harder) to scan from varying distances. The smaller the individual squares that make up the full QR Code the harder it is to scan at distance or in low light.

- Un-shortened QR Code: scanned at a maximum distance of 10 inches from the printed QR Code

- Shortened QR Code: scanned at a maximum distance of 30 inches from the printed QR Code.

The un-shortened URL has more data to pack into the same image size; therefore the individual will need to be closer to it in order for the camera to pick out enough detail and for the scanner to decode. This, as you can imagine, is where the strength in a well-planned and carefully implemented QR Code will come – make the QR Code as large as possible, with a good resolution, to enable a greater range of successful scanning.

You try it, using the two different QR Codes – how close or far from each do you have to be until your default or preferred scanning App can read and decode them?

There is a very useful blog called QRWorld (run by Eismann O'Reilly) that, in 2011, wrote a great analysis of the different uses for QR Codes and scanning distances.

http://goo.gl/R9APu
QR Codes Scanning Distance

Here Eismann broke the intended uses for QR Codes into the following 'categories':

- *Intimate*: magazines, newspapers, post / fliers, menus, books, DVDs, etc.

- *Personal*: shop signs, timetables (train, bus, etc.), museum, etc.

- *Social*: club / pub posters, shop window displays, etc.

- *Public*: billboards, T-shirts, side of buildings, etc.

Again, consider where you will be displaying your QR Codes – classroom wall poster, library book cover, presentation slide, school window, etc. and where your expected scanner will be stood. How big do you need to make the code in order for it to be a viable and successful scan from the distances you can expect your audience to be?

Creating QR Codes

The list below is by no means a full or comprehensive list of websites to use, but these are ones I use or have used in the past.

Note: All of these QR Code generating websites are, at the time of writing, free to use.

Kawya: http://qrcode.kaywa.com/
The first and most basic of the generators I've used, and still a firm favourite. Most other QR Code generators concentrate on only web addresses but this still give you the ability to create QR Codes for web addresses, plain text message, phone number, SMS (number and pre-defined message content), or contact details.

Snap.vu: http://snap.vu/
This free QR Code generator will create your shortened URL and QR Code, all at the same time. The statistical tracking is basic but at least you can see how many times each QR Code has been scanned, on what date, and from what platform.

The biggest advantage of using Snap.vu is that the generated QR Code image also comes pre-prepared with the shortened URL as part of the image; you don't have to manually edit or add the text beneath the image and make it. The downside of this however is that the shortened URL does not look like a URL to the uninitiated – whether it's because it doesn't have the recognisable http:// text or the .vu domain is not recognised (a .com address would possibly have solved this?) is up for debate.

snap.vu/f7y5

Goo.gl: http://goo.gl/

Not specifically a QR Code generator and tracker, this URL shortening service offers the by-product of a QR Code from the shortened URL with the added benefit of the Google analysis of clicks, scans, history, etc.

When you create a shortened URL with Goo.gl all you have to do is add ".qr" to the end of the link and you will get a 150x150 pixel QR Code. If you want to use the codes and need them larger, as we often do, then you'll need a larger QR Codes than Goo.gl initially provides you with. This is how:

When you view your QR Code, as created by Goo.gl, the full URL in your browser address bar will have a whole lot of code in it, like this:

Change the section that reads 150x150 (the pixel size of the QR Code) to something larger – up to a maximum of 540x540. You then get a larger QR Code that will give your scanning audience a larger QR Code (and therefore a clearer and 'cleaner' scan) which will work from further away:

Delivr.com: http://delivr.com/
Apart from the Goo.gl system this is my most favourite one for creating QR Codes, and one I have used the most. The QR Codes are downloadable in PNG, JPG, EPS, or SVG file formats and, when scanned, will store location and device information for plotting in a fairly good tracking report.

QR Code

You have the choice to download your QR Code with or without your username as part of the URL embedded in the QR Code. Not sure which to choose? No worries. Both codes work the same way.

With Username
http://hopkinsdavid.delivr.com/1iom6_qr

Download as: PNG | JPG | EPS | SVG

Without Username
http://delivr.com/1iom6_qr

Download as: PNG | JPG | EPS | SVG

Advanced

These advanced settings allow you to modify the default settings that follow best practices.

URL	Without Username
Error Correction	L - Approx 7% (default)
Margin	4 blocks (default)
Scale	3X (default)
Code Color	000000
Background Color	FFFFFF

Download as: PNG | JPG | EPS | SVG

Image source: Delivr.com website

Visualead: http://www.visualead.com/
Take your QR Code one step further than the basic black and white squares. Upload an image (brand logo) and have the QR Code created around and within it. Here are two examples I created using my Twitter avatar (cartoon character) and LinkedIn profile picture. Each QR Code is created with a Visualead-specific shortened URL of my main blog address which, to gain access to the advanced statistics and support, require a registration and payment plan (there is still the free option which I used).

The full-size version are both scannable and valid QR Codes (I tried with several apps, all could make it work).

81

Images of Visualead QR Code examples.
Image source: David Hopkins http://goo.gl/F9Jim

Unitag: http://www.unitaglive.com/qrcode
If you have time and knowledge of Photoshop then you can create artistic and wonderfully colourful QR Codes (see QR Code Campaigns that worked) but, if you're like me and don't then this website will help you create something almost as nice, but certainly very colourful.

Image of Unitag QR Code example.
Image source: David Hopkins http://goo.gl/pwgx7

If you want to take advantage of the fuller range of features and statistical tracking available you will need to sign up for one of the paid options, but I created the one above, using my Twitter avatar, for free.

Printing QR Codes

One of the biggest mistakes I see is the positioning of a QR Code in an obscure, out of the way, corner of a poster or book or magazine advert, in such a small size that unless you have your scanner / phone levelled about 2 inches from the page it won't scan. And that doesn't even cover the impact a glossy paper finish can have. You must consider where the QR Code will be printed, and where that printed poster, paper, magazine, etc. will be read / scanned in order to maximise its potential.

My recommendations are:

- Leave a good amount of white space around the edge of the QR Code. This helps your scanning App to focus and determine the different between surrounding 'noise' and the QR Code itself. By and large I leave between 20-25% the width of the QR Code again around the edge.

- If you can edit the QR Code image and place the shortened URL in the image itself you have more control of how it is displayed and where, especially if you include it on a poster or something with some design 'flair'. This is my personal preference, but not essential to using QR Codes or whether they work.

- If you can't edit the image of the QR Code itself to put the shortened URL on, make sure you put the URL close to (ideally below) the QR Code. This is easy to do in Word or PowerPoint, or other s

- Don't make them too small, or too big. Consider the QR Code as part of your poster design, for example, and integrate it from the start. Don't add it at the end and then struggle to make room for it. If you're going to put a QR Code in your presentation slide then consider your audience and size of auditorium – make it as big as possible so the person at the back can still scan it.

- Explain what it is and what your audience is expected to do with it. Not everyone knows what a QR Code is, so tell them, and not everyone knows they'll need a dedicated App on their device to scan and decode it. On my poster for the 2012 QR Code workshop I placed the text "Scan me to find out more about the QR Codes in Higher Education workshop".

http://goo.gl/9o0GM
2012 HEA QR Code workshop

- Wherever you put the code you should also put the web address (if it indeed points to a web address) for those who don't have a QR Code scanner, or want to scan your QR Code.

- Explain what the audience can expect to get when they scan the QR Code – and make it worth it. If you can give them discount to a student club or student-run event, tell them. If they can gain access to a resource or game that is only available through the QR Code then make it sound great. If it is part of a QR Code scavenger hunt then let them know that if they miss just one QR Code they might miss some important direction or information that could affect their performance and completion.

Monitoring QR Codes

As I've highlighted above, some websites that will help you create your QR Codes can also give you statistical tracking of their performance. While this may not be important with a class of 20 – 30 children, you may find it useful to see when your QR Codes are being scanned (was it during class or at 3AM?). If your QR Code was shown in the last slide after your class left the room did all scans happen then or are your students sharing the QR Code by other means for students who didn't attend?

Monitoring your QR Codes is only important if you want to know these kinds of details.

Another added benefit of using a shortened URL service, whether it's from Google or others like http://bit.ly or http://owl.ly, is that if you add a "+" symbol to the end of the link you are able to view the clicks, views, and interactions that have been made on any web link in this book – e.g. http://goo.gl/P93fv+ will give you the statistics for the Goo.gl shortened URL for the page on my blog dedicated to this book. You can see the number of clicks or scans, the browser used to view the content, where the user came from (referrer) and what country they are in.

These interactions, from the Goo.gl system, are open and public. If you see anyone else using a Goo.gl shortened URL you can apply the same technique of adding the "+" to the end of the link and see the statistics for their campaign/link too.

Screenshot of Goo.gl shortened URL statistics.
Image source, David Hopkins

YOUR QR CODES

As we've seen in the previous chapter the biggest reasons a QR Code fails, or its perceived failure, is the awareness or uptake of the technology in general, but classrooms and education could be seen as a 'closed door' environment where you have the ability to inform and educate your target audience about QR Codes and how to use them. This should mean that the way you use your QR Code will work: after all, you have something the marketing department of a large multinational corporation doesn't have ... a captive audience!

Where can you use QR Codes?

Well, you can use them anywhere you want, for any reason, and don't let anyone else tell you otherwise. There are obviously instances and circumstances where a QR Code is not necessarily appropriate or the best method of getting information across, and there are times when it is totally appropriate – only you can be the judge of that.

The following examples build on the earlier list of examples of where QR Codes are already being used. As always, try your QR Codes out before releasing them on your audience: the one thing you don't want is a bad experience if your QR Code point to the wrong resource. You will also need to get other stakeholders involved in the process – there's no point in creating a QR Code campus tour or adventure game if the Estates Group remove them thinking it's some form of graffiti.

Classroom / Learning:

Resources – QR Codes pointing to an online or digital edition of the paper edition the students are working or interacting with. These can either be the same document or resource, just in electronic form, or expanded or further resources to enhance the learning experience of the topic, subject, or project.

Presentation slides – if you make your presentation slides available to students through your institution's VLE, or you've loaded them to websites like SlideShare, then produce a QR Code and place that QR Code on your final slide. Your students can scan the QR Code as they exit the auditorium and have access to your slides quickly and easily. Be careful if you link to files or resources that require a login to access, not all reader Apps will handle login pages and cookies the same way. As always, try your QR Codes out first before asking students to interact with them.

Hand-outs – If you provide paper hand-outs for lectures, seminars, or classroom activities consider using QR Codes to direct students to an online version and / or to further resources you want the students to have access to.

http://goo.gl/Z5I5R
Hand-outs: A5 sized double-sided postcards/handouts
supporting workshop & training

In 2012 I developed some postcards that I handed out during training sessions on Turnitin for online assessment and feedback, each one with a QR Code linking to a video supporting the training session.

Video – If you show a video during a presentation, or want your students to watch something but don't want to take the time out of your lesson or lecture, use a QR Code they can scan after the time with you and watch in their own time. This could be displayed in your presentation slides, hand-outs, poster, etc.

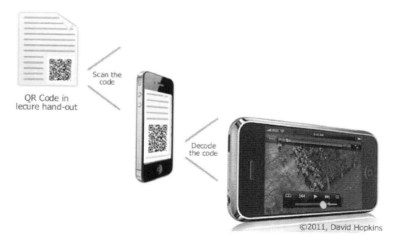

http://goo.gl/SLlhA
Video: Link to video through QR Codes

Orientation / Induction – QR Codes that form part of an orientation or induction activity can help students find their way around. Provide clues in each QR Code as to where the next one can be found, and the new students have to question and learn their way around a new or different physical environment. You could also use this methodology (with or without the QR Codes) for online induction activities.

Surveys – If your students need to survey each other then, instead of lots of students wondering around asking questions and possibly being annoying get them to produce a simple flier they can give out with a QR Code and short explanation on what the survey is about. This will then let the interviewee take the survey when they are ready. Note: make sure the survey is available in a mobile-friendly format before starting this.

Student work – If your students create their own work for projects, assignments, or posters then why not get them to record a short video or audio of them introducing it, and create a

QR Code they can place on the work itself for you and their classmates to scan and watch / listen to? Using the information in this book you can help them create the QR Code, place it in their work, and train them on how to use and scan the QR Code. They don't have to link to a video, they could quite easily link to their personal or class blog where the background work and research is identified and presented.

Bookmarks – Students print or save copies of QR Codes for websites they've visited and liked as a way to catalogue and preserve their work and investigations.

http://goo.gl/lNy5gB
Bookmarks: Classroom Bookmarks

Assignments - The University of Bath are using QR Codes as part of the assignment submission process. The student downloads their assignment submission coversheet from the VLE and the system dynamically assigns a unique QR Code to that student, for that particular assignment. When the student submits the paper copy of the assignment the QR Code is scanned which initiates a process of data capture of the student submission, date and time of scanning, and a receipt is generated and sent to the student informing them their assignment has been logged in the system as received.

http://goo.gl/rk8pu
Assignments: University of Bath: QR Code
Assignment Cover Sheet

Coursework – Use QR Codes to link to student work from previous cohorts or groups which are considered worthy of showing to the students as examples of good or notable work. This could be links to images loaded to Flickr of the students work, links to YouTube or Vimeo for video homework, SoundCloud for audio recordings, or DropBox for written assignments.

Contact hours – Place a QR Code on your door plate so students and parents can see your office hours and, if linked to an online Calendar service, book a meeting with you.

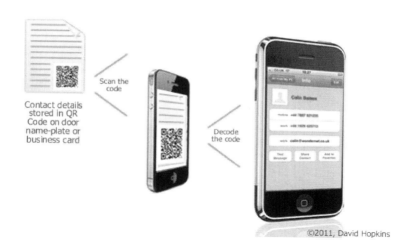

Contact details stored in QR Code on door name-plate or business card

Scan the code

Decode the code

©2011, David Hopkins

http://goo.gl/SLlhA
Contact Hours: Contact Details via QR Codes

Get help – QR Codes can link to all sorts of information, not just web addresses. You could use them to generate SMS messages or emails that will help the students find help on all sorts of topics (projects, learning, reading, etc.)

Support – Whatever support materials you produce, paper or electronic, there is always scope to link to two together. Paper versions are limited to the size of the printed edition, therefore you need to be very concise and exact with the information you include. The electronic resources can be far more involved and include multimedia resources, so why not link them with a QR Code.

This A3 sized poster I developed to support monthly 'hot desk' visits to different departments. The online resources contain more information about the kind of work, support, and training available as well as dedicated training hours for busy colleagues.

http://goo.gl/BpDBO
Support: Learning Technologist A3 Poster

Augmented Reality Games (ARGs) – Enhance the real world with an ARG and incorporate QR Codes to define story context, expose learners to characters and their point of view, and to guide discovery activities to further the story and game. This infographic by Gary Hayes illustrates how QR Codes can be integrated in to the ARG:

http://goo.gl/bESvuV
Gary Hayes: TranSocialMedia Story
Telling Workshop Sheet

Library

Shelves – Using QR Codes on the shelf can be useful, but it depends on what information you encode in the QR Code, and what the students can expect from it. Use the QR Code to link from the physical book shelf to the online catalogue where students can search for books and books on similar or related topics, reserve books online, read reviews, leave feedback, contact a librarian, ask for help, etc.

Books / Textbooks – Place a QR Code on the cover or inside the cover that links to the catalogue page for the book or textbook for further reading or similar titles. If you have students writing book reviews then why not have the QR Codes direct the scanner to the review that introduces the book, the characters, the background, a critical review of the work, the author, the historical context, etc.

http://goo.gl/9blHr
Books: Around the World in 80 Days
with 2D (QR) Codes (video)

Citation - Scan the QR Code on the paper cover to access a fully formatted and correct citation which you can save/download to other smartphone Apps like Evernote or DropBox.

eBooks – Place a QR Code on the cover of the paper edition of a book or on the shelf where the book is located, that links to the eBook edition of the work. This could help in situations where the only copy is already loaded but the electronic version is available.

The University of Bath have put QR Codes in the library catalogue, individual books and journal titles and on the shelves will, when scanned, save the title, author, and class mark of the resources. This is designed to help students find the resource and shelf location. The University of Bath have also put QR Codes on the floor plans enabling an audio tour of the floor and subjects available.

http://goo.gl/thCS8
eBooks: University of Bath: What is a QR Code?

Library / Subject blog – If you're library is running or maintaining a blog of research or new additions to the library database then place QR Codes at the check-out desk to highlight its value for information on scanning services, reservation details, out-of-print books, etc.

Instructional videos – If your library has developed, or has access to, video detailing what help is available then a strategically placed QR Code can highlight them. Example of this could be using the catalogue search features, check-out machines, room or computer booking, etc.

Student Group

Story telling – Use a QR Code to point students to a Google document where they are required to add a further line to the story at each visit. See how the story develops over time.

Julian Wood has developed this great video on how to stimulate storytelling using QR Codes, and it is worth watching if you can:

http://goo.gl/gjlG3G
Stimulating storytelling using QR Codes

Notes – QR Codes on notebooks or project files linking to the VLE or group blog / wiki to remind and enhance the experience of the group work.

Study Groups – Use QR Codes on noticeboards to highlight time and place of next study group or study support.

Student Union – Link posters and representative details to online versions where you have more room for more detailed descriptions of policies, responsibilities, contact details, office terms, voting systems, etc.

Conferences or Events

Business cards – If you have the ability to create or print your own business cards then a QR Code can link to your contact details, website or blog, class blog, list of journal articles or books, etc. If you, like many in large schools or Universities, have them printed for you, then why not print some sticky labels and put them on the back? I did this for the eAssessment Scotland Conference in 2011 and left them alongside my poster.

http://goo.gl/H8hei
Business Cards: 2011 eAssessment
Scotland Conference

Posters – Why not produce your lovely conference poster with a QR Code that links to a version loaded to your website, blog, or SlideShare? Now your audience can scan the QR Code and take a copy of the poster away with them for a more detailed examination on the train home. If you link to your research paper from the QR Code the audience has a more in-depth and detailed analysis of the poster's contents as well as a resource to interact with.

Presentation slides – see the explanation above of how QR Codes can be used in presentation slides. Using QR Codes at the end of your presentation enables delegates to scan it on their way out of the session and on to the next and can, depending on what you've linked to, download your presentation slides, view your LinkedIn or professional profile, connect with you through your blog or own website. The possibilities here are ones you ought to consider as part of managing your professional profile and 'brand'.

Advertising – Let's not get completely bogged down in the educational use. If you're planning to run a conference or event then why not use QR Codes on promotional materials, linking to the event website, list of speakers, booking details and form, network opportunities, etc. I did this for the 2012 HEA funded QR Code Workshop.

http://goo.gl/9o0GM
Advertising: 2012 HEA funded QR Code Workshop.

Badges – Put a QR Code on your conference or event badge, linking to your blog, LinkedIn profile, Twitter account, phone number, email address, etc. and let other delegates scan it for a record of whom you are and who they met on the day. Of course this does mean someone pointing their phone at your chest, which not everyone is comfortable doing (or having done to them).

ABOUT DAVID HOPKINS

David Hopkins

Thank you for getting this far, and for buying this book. I hope you have read or seen something here that has given you an idea (or two) on how QR Codes could help enhance or engage your students in a way that is either unique or different. I have provided lots of links and content and examples for you, to help explain what I mean as well as to provide an environment that contextualises the message or purpose.

Please, please, please leave a review of the book on the platform you bought it from (Amazon, iTunes, Kobo, Smashwords, etc.) for others to know how the book has helped you. Please also share the book through your networks, (Twitter, Facebook, Google+, etc.) to help spread the good news about QR Codes in classroom environments.

David Hopkins, May 2013.

David Hopkins' Bio:

From 10 years' experience as a Web Designer and Internet Consultant David has developed a respected reputation as a Learning Technologist. From 5 very productive years at the Business School, Bournemouth University, he joined the University of Leicester in May 2012. Using his background and experience with emerging Internet communication technologies David has been applying himself to Technology Enhanced Learning (TEL) and his work in areas of technology & pedagogical research.

Through his work, with both campus and distance learning students, David has used his experiences as a Learning Technologist to develop the use of QR Codes to link the printed, paper-based world of learning materials to the growing digital and online world of the computer-, laptop-, tablet- and smartphone-connected students. He has developed a reputation as a champion of QR Codes in Higher Education: he was instrumental in developing and managing several projects at Bournemouth University that used and investigated the use of QR Codes and, through his own personal research stream, developed a series of resources and blog posts on QR Codes and their applied uses in Higher Education, in and out of the classroom. In 2012 David, along with colleagues, gained funding from the Higher Education Academy in the UK and delivered a workshop that would take delegates on a "journey of discovery, tailored to their own QR Code experience".

Now working at the University of Leicester, one of the UK's top 20 Universities, he concentrates his work on aspects of technology and how it can be applied to current teaching practices as well as developing new ways to use existing and emerging technologies, both in and out of the classroom environment.

David shares his thoughts, research, work, conference & event reports, etc. on his Technology Enhanced Learning Blog 'Don't

Waste Your Time' www.dontwasteyourtime.co.uk and shares this and much, much, more through Twitter (@hopkinsdavid), LinkedIn (David M Hopkins) and other online networks.

http://goo.gl/H4tbH
David Hopkins (@hopkinsdavid) on Twitter

http://goo.gl/ZoEaD
David M Hopkins on LinkedIn

What is a Learning Technologist?

My journey as a Learning Technologist started in 2007 and has taken many turns and overcome many obstacles. What has remained throughout is the question of 'what is a Learning Technologist'?

Looking at published work and personal experience I have collected my blog posts together in this book and added further commentary and notes to provide the background to the posts and the work I am engaged in."

Available now in eBook format from Amazon, Kobo, and Smashwords for $0.99 / £0.69.

8603745R00061

Printed in Great Britain
by Amazon.co.uk, Ltd.,
Marston Gate.